SHOVING OFF *from the* SHORE

OTHER BOOKS BY LINDA KEEN

The Dream Keepers

Intuition Magic: Understanding Your Psychic Nature

John Lennon in Heaven: Crossing the Borderlines of Being

SHOVING OFF
from the
SHORE

poems

LINDA KEEN

Keen Press
California

Copyright © 2022 by Linda Keen
Printed in the United States of America

ISBN 13 (Paperback): 978-1-7333404-4-1
ISBN-13 (eBook): 978-1-7333404-5-8

All rights reserved. No part of this publication may be reproduced, stored in a retrieval system, or transmitted, in any form or by any means, electronic, mechanical, photocopying, recording, or otherwise, without the prior written permission of the author.

Keen Press
www.keenintuition.com

Cover Artwork by Oleg Stepanov

Author Photo by Ken Hassman

Book Design by Bri Bruce Productions
www.bribruceproductions.com

For my parents.

Contents

Introduction i
Remembering 1
Clap Nine Times 2
I Give Them 3
Snakes. 4
This Is All The Space I Have. 5
Coat Racks 6
Nothing Moves Quite Like Her 7
Different Sources 8
Never Breathe For Them 9
How Much I Loved The Mornings 10
Through The Cracks 11
Throwing Pennies 12
Breathe 13
Skies Sleep 14
Hope's Frenzy 15
Buffalo Bill 16
Fire Child 17
Ain't 18
Rhythm 19
Fertile 20
Lunch 21

From This Black Stone 22
Once We Are There 23
Trains Pass Through Here 24
Underground Stream 25
Waiting 26
Moonlight 27
Groves 28
Bones 29
Ancient Floor 30
Be-Bop-A-Loo-A 31
Innocent Feet 32
Structures 33
Through The Eye Of A Needle 34
Four And Twenty Blackbirds 35
Pink Edsel 36
As The Sky Breathes 37
Trilogy 38
Forceps 39
Reptilian Brain 40
Their Birds Chirp 41
Future Crops 42
Sea Birds 43
Sodden 44
Entry 45
Take This Home 46

This Is All I Need	47
I Will Know You	48
The Space Between Us	49
Small Airplane	50
Pears On Small Trees	51
Take Up The Hark	52
Maybe	53
Moviegoers	54
Ashram	55
Hillocks	56
Face	57
I Sing Thee	58
Saint Francis	59
Wee Boat	60
About The Author	63

Introduction

In the first years of the new millennium, I was to discover an entirely new form of writing. I still don't know how it came about, but I suspect it had to do with the recent passing of both my parents. It was the first time in my life that I was forced to comprehend in depth what mortality might signify within the realm of my most rudimentary existence.

At this very same time, I had just received my master's degree and had begun working as a public school counselor in a large metropolitan city in California. It was the commencement of a new era in which, for the first time in my life, I realized how—in becoming responsible for some key elements in the public school system at large while working with other colleagues, bosses, and supervisors—I was being challenged and influenced in some very unexpected ways.

It had been second nature for me to

enjoy and support my students and their parents—to be literally in awe of them and their unique capacities, creativity, and often the innocence of their instincts—yet I was becoming progressively saddened. Because I was discovering how appallingly limited I felt in my ability to share playfulness, mirth, and heartfelt intentions with so many of my routinely serious and seemingly driven adult colleagues.

Hence, I couldn't seem to fall asleep at night anymore. So, I devised a system of sitting up in bed, often in the cold, with pen and paper in hand, allowing myself to scribble down an astonishingly endless stream of strange and sometimes amusing images I felt honored to be receiving. It appeared that writing prose was the only thing that could keep me sane. It was giving me new life.

This book is dedicated to both my remarkable parents from whom I am so fortunate to have acquired a sense of both playfulness and seriousness in equal measures. Their lives are sometimes reflected in these writings, and I have taken the title from the very last piece in this collection. It is something I wrote several days after the passing of my father who preceded my mother by just a couple of years in their sacred and elusive crossings.

Linda Ellen Keen
Independence, Oregon
January, 2022

SHOVING OFF
from the SHORE

Remembering

I am remembering what it was like to breathe. The house was safe. The floor was kind. Doors were open panes of big glass. The furniture wanted me, as well as the fishpond. An invisible piano stood at the doorway. I never learned how to play it.

Clap Nine Times

This is how it should be: we hold our hands up to the sun and clap nine times. I always told you that this was a special day. If we expand too quickly we might get displaced. And where would that put us? I'm waiting to dream about sea lions and distant memories of when I knew you in Africa. The sands were so hot then and the treetops swayed to the beat of my heart.

I Give Them

I give them to the leaf piles, orange and red. I give them to the cool mist and nudging breeze. I give them to the crows walking in the old street. I give them to the oak groves and the arms of all trees. I give them to the child who does not want to greet me. I give them to the small leaves falling on my lips. I give them.

Snakes

They are symbols for what I know. These lines are not human. They are black snakes moving in a lost world; I never knew how to stack them. My hand was not guided. I sit here waiting in the dark, where it doesn't matter if the snakes are called pretty or if some tribal chief gives them his blessings. They are symbols for what I know.

This Is All The Space I Have

On the back, this is all the space I have. Amid empty cardboard boxes and a four-year-old named Daniel, this is all the space I have. A blue plastic hippopotamus becomes lost in a sea of human souls. Searching for shoes and ski parkas with fake fur. This is all the space I have. My whole world fits on the back of a small white card.

Coat Racks

"I want to be cremated," she said, walking past the coat racks. "Not me," he answered her without turning. "It's all about learning how to live without fear," she sighed. "I think I saw this coat in the other store," he told her, taking it off the rack and holding it up for approval. "I'm going to put it in my will, I think it's important," she said firmly. "I think the color might be too dull..." he said.

Nothing Moves Quite Like Her

I wish it were that simple. She's a spoiled child carrying laurel wreaths. Her singing is so pure; it makes the whole village dance. She doesn't know how to do it otherwise. This is the beauty of anger. Nothing moves quite like her.

Different Sources

Cannot see in the shadow of my own hand. We need light from different sources. It is that simple. The sun and the moon. The stars. The center of our foreheads. Your eyes. My heart.

Never Breathe For Them

Never breathe for Them. Keep your chin high and your belly tucked. Don't leave the lights on. You'll never make it that way. Look smart. Turn inside, feel the small brown puppy. But don't let go of the steering wheel, you're going to need it.

How Much I Loved The Mornings

When the earth finally dies, we're gonna lose Shakespeare, Mozart and the Beatles. Stonehenge and McIntosh computers. God won't give a damn about all of this. But He will ask us what we learned. I think I will want to tell Him how much I loved the mornings, especially the ones in which birds sang to me from across the garden. He will ask me if It Was Worth It, and I will tell him I Think So Except I Wonder Why So Many People Had To Die. He will smile at me and tell me He is sorry.

Through The Cracks

Poetry is squeezed out through cracks in the wall. It is cold sitting here and sleep is its victim. I'm not willing to compromise. To hell with the soft pillows and warm legs. I'm gonna shine, Baby!

Throwing Pennies

The faucet turns and I smile at my wasted hours. When will the clocks decide to go home? They never were very kind. I can only learn to throw pennies into the upturned bowl and hope that someone, anyone, will notice.

Breathe

They don't teach people to breathe properly anymore. Have you noticed? When leaning out of a 12-story window, they just expect us to know the words to every song, the steps for every dance, without any preparation. I think I'll go back to school and become a jazz singer. I'll stand on two feet and let the lyrics soar.

Skies Sleep

Irritation is like a funny shirking of responsibility. You can turn away from the familiar kiss only to catch a basket full of words. You feel your openness and glance at your magical fingers wrapping around the pen as roots clasping a rock. This can make you really happy and then you go to sleep longing for purple heavens, radiant horizons and mysterious stars. These depths, these open skies sleep in your trees.

Hope's Frenzy

One more for the road before pink, churning innards begin to make big waves of excitement. Surely one's desire to rest will balance out this hysterical frenzy of hope. We are talking about the kind of hope that bathes infants in rivers of a sudden-turn-of-events. Something no one could even imagine possible. Purple banners and golden hoops begin to roll into town and I am inviting all my friends.

Buffalo Bill

When I look in the newspapers, I would swear that Buffalo Bill just got shot. They were telling me they weren't sure yet if he would live. Don't you think this is kind of depressing? Especially because we don't even know which page he lives on or what his real telephone number used to be. I can always call my waiter over here and ask him. Do you think he would know? This is a very serious matter. The world will be much the lesser if Old Buffy doesn't make it. I'm sure the funeral will be broadcast live throughout the civilized world, don't you think???

Fire Child

Cornstalks form the fragile skeleton of open fields. A farmhouse allows its ghosts to wink at the other falling structures, even the spirits of dogs and cats. Suspenders hold a lanky farmer who stands so straight and tall, he often becomes the beams of his own front porch. Sometimes he smiles and reaches down to pick up his fire-headed daughter and then hands her to his silent wife. The pigs, the chickens, a cow, a great bull. Fire child plays with them all. A black puppy, as she bends down. With skin white as milk, her gentle lips kiss the dark earth.

Ain't

It's much harder to describe rotten apples than the Garden of Eden. Why can't we just crawl back into that tree? A naked ape throws apples at his tormentor. He lies in the branches, hoping for sunlight and peace. He ain't gonna get it.

Rhythm

Darkness is a curtain of music I can't stand. Its beat makes my feet tap anyway. I can't stand it, this rhythm of doom.

Fertile

Peering out of the whole, the fecal dream makes its way into a cold world. Its warm bed of filthy pinkness will be lost forever. It will have to learn how to cope with Life As It Is. There's no looking back now. We say prayers around it and sing litanies of praise. Oh Lord, please turn this fertile piece into ground for new ways.

Lunch

I've hit my head against that wall so many times; I can see its atomic parts. So you want fewer tears and more Himalayan chutzpah, do you? Enough to melt down this silly goose carriage with feathers on top? You say I should stop wagging the tail and start wagging the dog? Well, how about all these spoiled dreams waiting to receive their new assignments? Don't you see I'm a sheep in lion's clothing? You say I'm a frigging mustard seed? How can I possibly believe you? I am fighting for my life in a world of my own making. Just look inside the refrigerator and you'll find it there: a leftover lunch in a dirty cloth bag.

From This Black Stone

Now it's time to breathe. You see far horizons lit with the fires of our breath. Hope and brilliance from this black stone. Do you run, strong soul? You kiss my eyes with your flames. My faith again grows. Oh break my heart—from this black stone you arise.

Once We Are There

This may be the last chance we'll get. Windows into the deep forest bring back blue rain. We can't live without it, this ecstasy moving at the speed of light. Trees wave at me. I can smell their birds and taste their roots. Once we are there, nothing else will matter. I stare at it from here, the best of both worlds.

Trains Pass Through Here

Trains pass through here all the time. They used to be guided by stars. Small girls would dress their dolls, oblivious to the ravages of time. Perfection existed within the domed cars, time would stand still. Adventure was born here, I won't cry for home.

Underground Stream

He sits in his earthen cave, legs crossed. He thinks of us, as an underground stream plays from underneath his divine form. Water seeks us and the depths of his eternal pool. His flame may come and go, the light always remains. Oh, darkness of brown, oh ruggedness of earth! Oh, enlightened pools— fill my heart with your gladness. I swim in your joy.

Waiting

I saw her little shadow on the door. Where the sun was shining, I saw her tiny fluttering wings amidst the leaves, trembling in the wind. Through the little window, the brilliance was a gift without warning, the creature peering in, looking for me, for all of us who would have her. From outside, her delicate green body searched our hearts, wanting to enter. We wanted to receive her, to let her come inside; then the pain of knowing it would kill her. I think of her now, hovering in the flower box, a distant friend, waiting to come in.

Moonlight

The moonlight illuminates my garden at midnight, I cannot ignore it. The migrating swans fly high overhead, their whiteness intensified, their calls take me up. Late November and roses still grow, supernatural beacons, I watch.

Groves

Drape these branches with my soul, Mother. Fly me on your wings, Father. The sky breathes me open into its vast circle, clear and crisp. I die in its arms. Carried through time, I may see. I remember these groves, they never left. Only the shapes around them have changed. They had to. We don't care; our tunes carry to those ears that are listening. They have always listened. I dare to sing here again, and again, and again.

Bones

I could go on and on. Our bones are scattered in the desert. Only one train runs through and it's heaving black smoke. On it is a girl going west, riding to her timely demise. While angels gawk, even the kiss of life from a saint cannot help her. I'm sorry, it is very sad. Yet few will cry. Only the spirits will rejoice at her homecoming. They always do. As the sun sets into the ocean, a dark haired master says prayers of salvation.

Ancient Floor

I seek an inn without sore music. Where the yearning hearth burns directly into my skin and lets me fall, drunken, onto an ancient floor. Full of mossy words where there are no aluminum window frames and fake leather chairs. Where no whining lyrics rape our ears, no processed air can steal our breath away. No deathly white light telling us we are lost. I seek an inn with the slight smell of human breath and fresh dung. Where light can live without suspicion. Where the hearth can burn all doubt from our hearts. Where our feet can rest. A place for old artists and young farmers. Where fiddles play themselves into a frenzy of self-assurance. Where a Christmas song can be sung outside on the streets. Where money is simple and streets are empty.

Be-Bop-A-Loo-A

This is not my idea of a good time. The wine is sour and so are the notes. I thought I could escape into a soft bubble of truth, but my joy has popped. Only "Be-Bop-A-Loo-A" can save my soul, John Lennon's return, a vague memory of when I saw him on that hill. Everything changes with it. The hideous illusion fades. I see those molecules of hope; feel the sun rising on my dirty apron as we enter the kitchen. Outside it is raining. Let's not forget this.

Innocent Feet

White concrete is covering the colors of your silky robes. When I blink, I see peaceful tigers walking in our direction. The damp earth shakes with sensual rhythm. Why must I turn to this cold, gray wall? With my eyes on the ground, the silver snakes wink at my innocent feet. Green grass offers us a bed. Why let the metallic caves eat at our radiance? The sound of bells takes me to your garden.

Structures

Strange days shake my temple to the ground. Of all being bricks collapsing. Feeble structures sickening heights to be attained. Is anyone in there? To be pulled from the rubble from within. My heart knows who this is.

Through The Eye Of A Needle

I have passed through the eye of a needle. I walk through the rain wearing my mother's bonnet. I see the very street where I remembered it was me. I was never happier; I hear the lullaby of drops on warm plastic, humming the harmony part, I breathe in sweet air. Rubber boots scuff the silver sidewalks of my solitude.

Four And Twenty Blackbirds

Today I became large. What a coincidence that it is your day of going away. I didn't let this make me sad. I only used it as an excuse to grow. I removed my hat and allowed four and twenty blackbirds to escape. Now there's nothing I can't do.

Pink Edsel

The ghost of Mr. Cunningham flies like a helicopter above my racetrack. He tells me not to give up, that help is on the way. The clouds reflect, blimp like, my state of grace. Over in the parking lot, his pink Edsel cruises softly in the ethers to the rapture of Handel's Violin Sonata in D Major.

As The Sky Breathes

If I would breathe like the sky, I would be able to float out the door and move with my warm humanity—all shaking with cold and loss—out the window and into the rain, filled with the tears of the dead. These souls in shock seek the last embrace of their loved ones, at the very least, a goodbye. But the sky did not allow them this chance and they were ripped from the arms of our earth, flung into the cosmic sea by a monster sea of life, by a divine order we do not understand. These voices I hear are not yet serene and they cry for their loved ones, for the familiar bed where mortal heads blissfully lie. Waiting for the sun to return, waiting for that last kiss. But it will not come to them now and they lie, instead, in the cold bed of the sea, waiting to breathe again as the sky breathes.

Trilogy

I.

Sweet, sticky cake goes down the choked throat of a goodbye; while downstairs, a witch's brew threatens long term poisoning. Here upstairs, friends can hold a hand over their heart and say thank you. Downstairs, the darkness is laughable. Yet, in the morning, I must return again and again to face my movable feast of belly churning fate. Which shall it be? The aqua blueness of blissful flight? Or, the sick red flames of that hollow voice?

II.

I sit here knowing that my aching seat on the precipice is soon to eject me into the rightful pulse of an imploding dance.

III.

I rejoice in mid-air.

Forceps

I have succeeded in the agonizing task of entering the world anew. There were the searing forceps and major disappointment of no perceivable parents to greet me. Yet, I transported myself, all red and slippery, to the back room of a quiet, foreign apartment building, transposed into the sturdy practical arms of a perfect aunt (herself childless) and into a hush of common bliss. They weren't aware of me, but I of them. I thanked my twin for the blessed reception. Only he knew, then, that our teacher was superimposed onto the wallpaper tapestry. He knew these soft orange robes would one day comfort us both. Both of us, healed by the whispered words of unspeakable love. In the early morning light, the father and the mother reclaimed their sacred bond.

Reptilian Brain

It's hard to put your finger on it. Me, with a panicked invasion of the frontal lobes. They, carrying a bronzed version of the Magna Carta and charging my way. It's pitiful, really, how some people can never seem to grow up, while others were legislating new bills in Congress from the day they took their first breath. Funny how my reptilian brain works as a receptor site for the nighttime thrills of the jungle. You'd think the cage could be opened, one of these days. You'd think I would now be ready to receive the freedom offered to me from the start. You'd think I would fly into it as a dying person who sees her first glimpse of etheric light.

Their Birds Chirp

Mean people suck and kind people lose their positions. But they fight back in other ways. Their birds chirp loudly in the glittering sunlight's shadows. While hardness roams the streets, cold and hungry. Blessed are they who awaken early and sing on mountaintops. They shall inherit new songs.

Future Crops

I.

The hollow wooden bird has found her voice. It rings across the land, giving life to new sprouts. These future crops know her heart. They will feed her until the old woodenness decays into flesh and feathers made of dense light.

II.

When will you receive the conscious glimpse? The exquisite gift wrapped in soft, evil scarves? When will you grab their colors in your hands, fall down on the cold and cry out for your life? When will the barren trees crash down all around you and your frightened eyes? When will you look so deeply into madness, it makes the mountains cry?

Sea Birds

These words sometimes feel like sea birds caught in a storm. The wind sends their tiny bodies into the air, feathers eschew, fighting the chaos of sound. These words cry out, vanished in the thunderous foaming cold, carried far down the shore. There they wait safely behind jagged brown rocks, huddled together without thoughts.

Sodden

My raincoat lashed by wind and downpour, I thank these ragged cathedrals of ancient uproar. To be here now, sodden in the wisdom of their company, I intuit the world as it once was. This sea, these waves, these pools—fill and answer me, my soul so small and old.

Entry

Awaken at sunrise in a weathered cabin, new light blinding sheltered eyes. Simplicity of day staggers all thoughts. Inhale bracing air, feet on cold red stone floor. Thin wooden walls only separation from ocean smells and clamor of feathered angels. Running out the door in baggy clothes, just in time for first, piercing rays. From behind round, emerald hills, shooting gold. Inside children sleeping, dreaming of waves.

Take This Home

How do words take away ringing ears, aching flesh, time is up, no more judgment? They are the holy relics. Do you really believe you can wake up in the morning speaking the lines you wrote in your wildest dreams? Will you ever finish all those books written about words? I think I will see you answering these questions standing on your ship as the sun sets, saying your lines, oh yes, we will be free. Take this home and place it on the altar of your heart.

This Is All I Need

Sleep tumbles out of my body like a laugh at noonday. There are many ways to breathe tonight, I shan't be bothered. If only to hold the rose, the long stem, to feel its life burning in my hands, to gaze at its kindness, to smell its brilliance. This is all I need, my twin and I touching its soft thorns, not unaware of the burning world, not fearful of happiness. Knowing we are already dust, yet being the dark earth, its rain, its air.

I Will Know You

I will know you by your bare feet and smile.
I know it is you who has placed the bowl in
my hands, filled with fear. I emptied it slowly,
too carefully at times, but you would wait for
eternity as if it were the blink of an eye. Bless
this food I turn so slowly on my tongue, teeth
clamped onto the thick fibers of surrender.
Lead me there, take me from this dusty road,
tell me where is the grove.

The Space Between Us

Lightness dances in the shadows of this house, my eyes see only gold and green. Standing on the stairs, looking across the room, the space between us heaves a sigh. Reflecting particles of now, it is all I can do to collect it, to become the sun itself, to know I can stay. A few more steps downwards and the green turns into the blueness of your eyes.

Small Airplane

This is how it is: a small airplane humming me to sleep. It does not need much attention. In the morning, it will land like a butterfly on my fence, ready for the nervous flower. It does not matter if the sun will shine: love will guide it.

Pears On Small Trees

Can you remember how we played? The gentle street was youth's release. We never stopped looking for pears on small trees. Do you remember the dog's blue tongue? The rocks upon which we sat as big as a house? I turn toward your dirty tee shirt and worn brown shoes. I climb, once more, up the hill with you, a hot breath at my side. Your tomboy hair glints dark-amber in the sun, your freckled face squinting through stream blue eyes. How did I ever forget you?

Take Up The Hark

Tomorrow will be this new chance to live. It will eat my blind resistance, drive away the black hole, sink the ship of sameness. Shimmers of stable joy will bounce across every room as I bring the faeries back, take up the hark of blessed solitude, incorporate the tune. Moving will be liquid melodies, frames of organized conviction. I'll bid for my sanity and more. Tomorrow will be a new chance to live, a day of wildest design.

Maybe

Maybe I have lost you. Maybe you have lost me. Maybe we are swimming upstream together. Maybe we can see each other through cloudy eyelids and tangled hair. Maybe we are tired of the finned fight. Maybe we see that sandy shore in the sunlight. Maybe we could meet there, where mermaids have fought cold seas to get here. Maybe we are just waiting.

Moviegoers

There are better images waiting. Like impatient moviegoers behind the strain of shadows, in the old theater, I remembered. Neither time nor space can make our loss addiction invalid. Only the sun can blind us to the pain upon reentering.

Ashram

Inside of me live my mother and father and all the generations. I carry them inside the ashram of my heart.

Hillocks

The stars are endless and I have traveled this far. I seek my return to that emerald knoll, the hearth amidst the village auld. A hut amidst the bramble rows. The only place to live and dream—in these green hillocks where I lay down my soul.

Face

Cool white light of the moon speaks ghostly.
Embodied daylight brings warmth to the dark
valleys of thought. I await the unspeakable
knowing. I long to see thy reassuring face!

I Sing Thee

I sing thee, as a white bird, I travel gracefully to thy warm nest of brownish straw. I nestle with the tiny eggs of speckled blue. I crouch down into safety in thy hands. I peer outward with all encompassing, staring eyes and the sound of silent winter skies.

Saint Francis

Oh Saint Francis, Santa Clarita! Oh blameless angels! Show me your path of compassion. Children of pain wait for your warm touch. Upon aching shoulders of old burdens, original sins are washed away. In rivers of love, you carry us along in your vessels of hope.

Wee Boat

He took his small boat yesterday, shoving off from the shores of mortality. On this long journey, he had forgotten his way home. Yet, gliding now out of the cove, he rows himself closer and closer to jubilation. He is at peace with the wind, even as strong waves lap his wee boat. Sunlight in his heart, I can hear him singing.

About The Author

LINDA KEEN is an American healer, author, and teacher of metaphysics, as well as a professional musician and former school counselor. She began her metaphysical practice in 1978 in the Netherlands after discovering her aptitude for using her intuition to help others. Providing support to clients looking for significant answers to questions concerning a soul's purpose in everyday life, Linda unwittingly pioneered an entirely new method of training within the Dutch self-help community.

The most striking realization Linda had in the course of her work was how each and every human being has full access to his or her own elaborate body of spiritual information—if only they have the interest required to seek and find it. This access is one of the lesser-known and/or acknowledged gifts of the remarkable human psyche. As many now know, the gift of the imagination is truly the most powerful tool we humans possess in determining our ability to "be still and know," and it remains the primary source of all our self-healing.

Although Linda has been writing poetry, prose, and song lyrics of her own compositions since the age of fifteen, this book of prose is Linda's first published offering outside the realm of her metaphysical writings and teachings.

She is excited to share this aspect of her lifetime's imaginative journeys with you, perhaps stirring up those untapped aspects of yourself in which unassuming daydreams and imaginings are given full permission to take on a life of their own.

Linda's books in English include, *Intuition Magic: Understanding Your Psychic Nature* (1998, 2019); *John Lennon in Heaven: Crossing the Borderlines of Being* (1993, 2019), and *The Dream Keepers* (2016, 2019), her first young adult novel.

Linda has been featured on national television and radio as an author (including

NPR's All Things Considered in 2000) and has written a total of seven books, two of them illustrated children's books published in the Netherlands in the Dutch language.

In the words of Dr. Seuss, who shares the same day of birth as Linda (March 2nd): "Be who you are and say what you feel, because those who mind don't matter and those who matter don't mind."

"Integration of all that we know and can accomplish" remains Linda's mission.

Learn more about Linda and her work at www.keenintuition.com.

www.ingramcontent.com/pod-product-compliance
Lightning Source LLC
Chambersburg PA
CBHW051701040426
42446CB00009B/1238